W9-AMB-664

FIVE Little MONKEYS

bake a birthday cake

Eileen Christelow

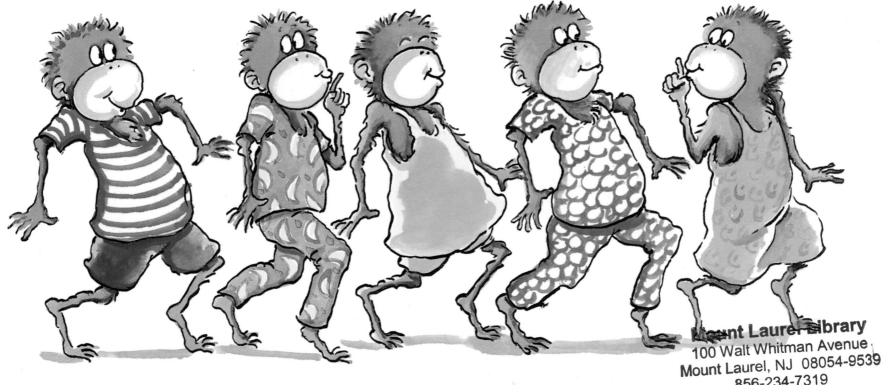

Clarion Books • New York

For Bob, Karen, and Liza

Clarion Books
a Houghton Mifflin Company imprint
215 Park Avenue South, New York, NY 10003
Copyright © 1992 by Eileen Christelow
Cover illustrations copyright © 2004 by Eileen Christelow

Originally published in 1992 under the title *Don't Wake Up Mama!*

The illustrations were executed in pen and ink and acrylic gouache.
The text was set in 16-point Kabel.

www.houghtonmifflinbooks.com

Printed in the U.S.A.

The Library of Congress catalogued the original hardcover edition as follows:
Christelow, Eileen.
Don't wake up Mama! : another five little monkeys story / Eileen Christelow.
p.   cm.
Summary: Five little monkeys try to bake a cake for their mother's birthday without waking her up.
ISBN 0-395-60176-2
[1. Monkeys—Fiction. 2. Cake—Fiction. 3. Baking—Fiction. 4. Birthdays—Fiction.] I. Title.
PZ7.C4523 Do   1992   91-45514
[E]—dc20
CIP
AC

CL ISBN-13: 978-0-618-49647-1   CL ISBN-10: 0-618-49647-5
PA ISBN-13: 978-0-618-49648-8   PA ISBN-10: 0-618-49648-3

WOZ   10 9 8 7 6 5 4 3 2 1

Five little monkeys wake up with the sun.
"Today is Mama's birthday!"

3

Five little monkeys tiptoe past Mama sleeping.

"Let's bake a birthday cake!"

4

"Sh-h-h! Don't wake up Mama!"

One little monkey reads the recipe.
"Two cups of flour. Three teaspoons of baking powder.

"Sift everything together.
But don't sneeze! You'll wake up Mama!"

"Sh-h-h! Don't wake up Mama!"

A-AHCHOO

Five little monkeys check on Mama.

"She's still asleep. We can finish making the cake."

One little monkey reads the recipe.
"Add four eggs."
Four little monkeys each get some eggs.

"And we need sugar and oil."
"Don't spill the oil!"

But one little monkey spills…

...And another little monkey slips and falls.
"Sh-h-h! Don't wake up Mama!"

Five little monkeys check on Mama.
"She's still asleep.
We can finish making the cake."

One little monkey reads the recipe.

"Next, mix everything together and put it into pans.

Then bake the cake in the oven."

16

Another little monkey says, "Now we can go up
to our room and make a present for Mama."

Five little monkeys start to make a present.
"Sh-h-h! Don't wake up Mama!"
One little monkey says, "Do you smell something burning?"

18

Five little monkeys race past Mama sleeping.
"Sh-h-h! Don't wake up Mama!"

"Oh no! The cake dripped all over."
"Turn off the oven!"
"Save the cake!"
"Sh-h-h! Don't wake up Mama!"

"Look! Here comes the fire engine!"
says one little monkey.
"Sh-h-h! Don't wake up Mama!"
says another little monkey.

"Wait!" says another little monkey. "This cake doesn't taste TOO bad." "Frosting might help," says the other fireman.

Five little monkeys and two firemen frost the cake.

"Now we can wake up Mama!"

Five little monkeys and two firemen
sing to Mama very, VERY, VERY LOUDLY.

29

And Mama wakes up!
"What a wonderful surprise," she says. "But my birthday is tomorrow!"

"Oh no!" say five little monkeys. "But can we still have birthday cake for breakfast?"

"Why not?" says Mama.

Five little monkeys, two firemen, and Mama think the birthday cake is delicious.

One little monkey whispers, "We can bake another cake tomorrow."

Another little monkey says, "Sh-h-h! Don't tell Mama!"